THE
BUSINESS WRITING
POCKETBOOK

By Clive Bonny

Drawings by Alan Roe

D0807715

"Bite-size messages with a big impact."
Mel Webb, Sector Skills Development Manager

"Informative and concise: good book, good words."
Richard Wolfstrome, Director, Advanced Media Associates

"Essential for reminding us that simplicity is the key to success."
Gilly Smith, Managing Director, Juicy Guide

"Sensible suggestions for delivering straightforward messages."
Keith Stafford, Training Editor, Reuters

CONTENTS

PLANNING 5
Choosing channels, 4 I's, costing,
3 R's, 5 W's, 7 C's, starting up

**INTERNAL
CORRESPONDENCE** 15
Memos, reports, minutes, e-mail,
desk messages, faxes

**EXTERNAL
CORRESPONDENCE** 31
Letters (layout, structure, examples,
courtesy, complaining, selling),
proposals (drafting, structure, format),
web sites

PERSONALISING 49
Language, style, tone, sexism,
personalities, VHF

PRESENTING 65
Charts, graphs and diagrams,
putting ideas on paper, mind-mapping,
handwriting

MARKETING COMMUNICATIONS 89
Stationery, strategy, direct mail,
advertising, press releases

CHECKING 105
Speed reading, jargon, clarity,
redundancy, grammar, clichés, spelling

INTRODUCTION

The purpose of business writing is to tell as much as needed for the reader as clearly and as quickly as possible.

The purpose of this Pocketbook is to improve your business writing skills quickly in planning, producing and checking.

This means that you will be able to:

- **reduce the time spent composing your messages**

- **choose the most appropriate expressions for different situations**

- **make it easier for readers to understand you**

- **enhance your image in the eyes of your readers.**

INTRODUCTION

QUOTATIONS
"WE ARE WHAT WE WRITE"

"The last thing we decide in writing a book is what to put first."
Blaire Pascal 1623-1662

"The art of writing is the art of applying the seat of the pants to the seat of the chair."
Mary Vorse 1880

"There are three difficulties in authorship: to write anything worth the publishing, to find honest men to publish it and get sensible men to read it."
Charles Cotton 1780-1832

THE 90 : 90 RULE
90% OF LASTING IMPRESSIONS ARE MADE IN THE FIRST 90 SECONDS

REMEMBER TO MAKE AN INITIAL IMPACT:
THERE IS NO SECOND CHANCE TO CREATE A FIRST IMPRESSION

PLANNING

CHOOSING CHANNELS

- Is writing the right thing to do?
- Should you write, telephone or meet?

Deciding on **HOW** you send your message is the first step.

Exercise

Choose your order of preference: would you write (W) telephone (T) or meet (M) in these situations? You are:

1) advising a major customer of a significant delivery delay
2) confirming receipt of a large order
3) changing an important procedure at work for your team
4) recommending an unusual and possibly risky business opportunity to your boss
5) turning down a staff request for a pay rise.

See next page for recommended responses.

CHOOSING CHANNELS

- **Writing is best when there is a need for:**
  no immediate feedback
  an accurate legal record
  complex information and detail.

- **Telephoning is best when there is a need for:**
  some immediate verbal feedback
  quick one-off issues
  simple facts.

- **Meeting is best when there is a need for:**
  immediate verbal and non-verbal feedback
  demonstration and observation of facts and feelings
  sensitive and confidential information.

Recommended responses
1) **Telephone or meet to explain, then write to confirm.**
2) **Telephone to thank, then write to confirm details.**
3) **Write to clarify and meet to explain.**
4) **Write then submit face to face.**
5) **Meet to explain.**

(7)

PLANNING

THE FOUR I'S

Define your **PURPOSE** and stick to it.
Your writing will need to achieve one of the four I's:

Instruct : eg: new policy or procedure
Inform : eg: advise progress
Interpret : eg: summarise details
Influence : eg: persuade to buy

Your purpose in writing should be clearly stated in your opening.

AVOID THE SLOW BUILD-UP - IT FRUSTRATES BUSY PEOPLE

PLANNING

COSTING

Professional services (eg: banks and solicitors) can charge you £25 - £50 for a single letter.

A stamp and stationery are less than **2%** of the cost.
98% of the cost is the **TIME** it takes to:

- research and plan the content
- layout and compose the draft
- write and check the copy

People involved can include managers, secretaries and mailroom assistants.

Overheads can include office space, filing cabinets, computers and franking machines.

Your correspondence costs you more than you think.

AVOID THE THREE R'S

Rush = Return = Re-write

Plan time to get it right first time based on your previous experience.

Don't underestimate the time needed for first drafts.

Allow up to **THREE TIMES** longer to plan than to write.

PLANNING

THE FIVE W'S

WHO is it for? Keep the **reader** in mind

WHY are you writing? Make an early statement of **purpose**

WHAT will you say? Keep it short and simple (KISS)

WHERE will your main points go? Have a logical **flow**

WHEN do they need it by? Write in **time**

(and HOW long will it take you?) **BUDGET CONTINGENCY TIME!**

THE SEVEN C'S

A lways
Be

COURTEOUS	:	in tone, personalised to your reader
CONSISTENT	:	in format, layout and 'house' style
CLEAR	:	with visuals which are easy to read
CHECKED	:	spelling and use of English
CORRECT	:	facts and figures
CONCRETE	:	specific and descriptive words and phrases
COMPREHENSIVE	:	covering all you need to say and no more.

GETTING STARTED

OVERCOMING WRITER'S BLOCK

Problem:
Writer's Block happens when we are on the starting block and can't move.

Solution:
Start anywhere! You can sort out the logic later.
Get the words flowing, and don't stop to re-write as you go.

Your brain is stimulated more easily by words on paper than by your 'mind's eye'.

GETTING STARTED

- Outlining a false start is a first step
- Invest time outlining a draft
- Brainstorm random words and phrases
- Reassemble and link
- Prioritise
- Rewrite
- Do it before dictating

INTERNAL CORRESPONDENCE

MEMORANDA

Memos are similar to letters and similar guidelines will apply to both. The main differences are that memos are internal within organisations and are less formal. Less formality means memos can be shorter (ideally one page, but avoid being curt) and even handwritten.

Example Format:

DO

- Put your most important points first, in logical sequence, especially who it is for, why you are writing and what are the outcomes.

- Use headings, lists and pictures when possible.

- Check it carefully afterwards for clarity.

MEMORANDUM

TO:
FROM:
DATE:
SUBJECT:
MESSAGE:

SIGNED:

INTERNAL CORRESPONDENCE

REPORTS

Organisations make important decisions on the basis of reports.
Ineffective reports result in ineffective decisions.

Report writers are therefore often exposed to harsh scrutiny by both
bosses and clients.

Reports fall into 2 categories

ROUTINE : To inform of progress (usually internal)

SPECIAL : To instruct, inform, interpret or influence.

REPORTS

SPECIAL REPORTS need special planning.

Failing to plan is planning to fail.

C heck with the commissioner or receiver the deadline, purpose, scope, readership and resources available.

I dentify what information exists and is needed, who can help and where to go.

D raft subjects and headings, logically, with the main points first. Facts and figures must support conclusion and recommendations.

- Allow more time to plan, revise and edit than actual time to write.

- Finish proof-reading by reading aloud - one sentence should not be more than one breath.

(18) • Then 'sleep on it' if it's sensitive, and re-read.

REPORTS

- Clear 'signposting' is crucial.

- Headings should be in logical order, explicit and brief.

- Paragraphs should be numbered, with sub-paragraphs marked alpha-numerically
  eg: 3a   then
        3a (i) with further headings indented

  or   3.1   decimally, then
        3.1.1 in logical sequences

INTERNAL CORRESPONDENCE

REPORTS
BASIC LAYOUT

Remember: busy managers like summaries first!

1) **SUBJECT TITLE** (up to 10 words) and author's name
2) **INTRODUCTION** (up to 100 words) Purpose, scope and background
3) **SUMMARY** (up to 300 words) Main conclusions, recommendations, costs and cost-benefits
4) **RESEARCH METHOD** (up to 50 words) How information was collected
5) **FINDINGS**
   Facts and figures in order of importance
6) **CONCLUSIONS** (up to 100 words) based on findings
7) **RECOMMENDATIONS** (up to 300 words) Courses of action listing key points first
8) **APPENDICES**
   Supporting information with title headings cross referenced to contents page numbers. Include a glossary for jargon and bibliography if appropriate. Then bind it in a visually attractive way.

INTERNAL CORRESPONDENCE

REPORTS
OPTIONAL LAYOUTS

LESS FORMAL
For Letter and Memorandum Reports use only 3 stages:
- Purpose and Scope
- Situation and Findings
- Conclusions and Recommendations

MORE FORMAL
For reports involving major issues
ADD 3 stages
- Covering Letter : confirming the theme and giving thanks
- Contents Table : report title
  recipients' names
  author's name
  date
  headings and page numbers
  sub-headings
- Appendices : tables, graphs, charts, illustrations.

INTERNAL CORRESPONDENCE

MINUTES OF MEETINGS

- Minutes should be an accurate record of discussions held.
- Minutes can be taken by **any** person attending a meeting.

STANDARD FORMAT

Purpose, date, time, place
Names of Chairperson, attendees, absentees, minute-taker

Prior minutes approved

Matters arising from the Minutes

Agenda: first subject discussed ....
Actions agreed by whom, by when ....
Second subject discussed .... etc.

Any other business

Next meeting date and time

Circulation: As above names, plus .....

INTERNAL CORRESPONDENCE

MINUTES OF MEETINGS

TIPS

- Check in advance with the chairperson: the agenda, the format and the level of detail needed on record.

- Write in the third person, in the past tense, eg: 'The matter of AB Co was discussed. It was agreed that .....'

- Use numbered headings and underlining or **BOLD**.

- Identify individuals responsible for actions, and deadlines.

- Circulate after approval by the chairperson.

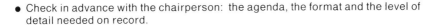

Meeting DATE .... TIME .... PLACE ....

PURPOSE .... CHAIR ....

PRESENT ....
....

ABSENT .... PAGE ....

ITEM No.	SUMMARY	ACTION	
		WHEN	WHO

MINUTED BY .... COPIED TO ....

NEXT MEET DATE .... TIME .... PLACE ....

SOUTHVIEW 8 STONEHILL CLOSE. EAST SHEEN. LONDON SW14 8RP
TELE (0181) 876-1454   FAX (0181) 878-6970

MINUTES
KEEPING TRACK

One method of recording discussion is to jot down comments as a **visual** record. These notes will then form the basis for preparing more formal minutes.

Example
To record dialogue where the chair is on your left, you are in the middle and others are on the right:

A. H. asked for
latest results

R. B. gave sales figures

I supplied
financial figures

A. H. reviewed
% new business

I gave forecasts

S. H. queried timescales

A. H. confirmed
timescales appropriate

INTERNAL CORRESPONDENCE

E-MAIL
POLICY ISSUES

Surveys reveal that one in three employees abuse e-mail:

- For political gain over colleagues (with blind copies)
- To avoid dealing personally with sensitive situations (when they should talk)
- To create a sense of self-protection (copying everyone)

Publish guidelines on using e-mail and have a clear e-mail policy that states:

- When employees can/cannot use the internet
- That offensive materials breach discipline
- What limits there are regarding private use
- Any monitoring procedures and why they're in place
- Penalties for breaching policy
- Procedures for revising policy

E-MAIL

DON'T WASTE TIME

If 10 people in a team each sends the other team members a weekly report for information purposes only, then each week the team members spend a combined 900 minutes reading reports. Over a year, this amounts to more than 100 working days!

Action:
- Screen-dump your inbox
- Count the time wasted on unnecessary info
- Tell the time-wasters!

INTERNAL CORRESPONDENCE

E-MAIL

HOW TO PRIORITISE E-MAIL

E-mail headers should state levels of importance and urgency.

Code each message with a level of importance, eg:

A = high
B = medium
C = low

Add a code for level of urgency, eg:

1 = reply within 24 hours
2 = reply within 72 hours
3 = reply unnecessary

DESK MESSAGES

HOW NOT TO

Have you seen something
like this on a handwritten note?

CHRIS CALLED YOU UNAVAILABLE
IMPORTANT TO CALL BACK
AS SOON AS POSSIBLE
WHEN NEARBY

CB

What do they mean?
BREVITY DOES NOT ALWAYS MEAN CLARITY
DON'T KICK OUT KEY WORDS OR FORGET PUNCTUATION

INTERNAL CORRESPONDENCE

ORGANISING FAXES

As with desk messages, use a pre-printed format.

Also

- Attach the fax confirmation slip (if available)
- Write in bold capitals (poor telephone lines can delete parts of words)
- Show your fax number to help replies
- Use coloured paper rolls to highlight incoming urgent messages
- Copy thermal paper onto plain paper for archive
- Avoid faxing OUT on dark coloured paper - it can take ten times longer to send

EXTERNAL CORRESPONDENCE

EXTERNAL CORRESPONDENCE

LETTERS

IMAGE

Your letters represent your personal and your organisation's image to the world outside - set high standards.

Keep your image consistent: where House Rules exist, follow them by applying the Seven C's (page 12).

EXTERNAL CORRESPONDENCE

LETTERS

LAYOUT

- Use letterhead stationery showing your location details. Quote your fax, phone and extension.
- Set a one inch margin. Double space between paragraphs.
  Start all text on the left margin. Put Day Month Year (no punctuation)
  eg: 13 May 1994 (Americans put Month Day Year).
- Use their name, title (if known) and full address (always spell-check carefully).
  Your Reference (for file purposes). Their Reference (from their prior letter).
- Salutation eg: Dear Ms Jones (where less formal).
                 Dear Madam   (where name is unknown).
- Subject heading: CENTRED IN BLOCK CAPITALS.
- Subscription or sign off: Yours sincerely (after named addressee).
  Yours faithfully (after Dear Sir or Madam).
- Sign it.
- Writer's name and title.
- Enclosure reference: Encl(s).
- Copies to: cc(s).

EXTERNAL CORRESPONDENCE

LETTERS
STRUCTURE

Always ensure that your letters follow a logical framework:

- Beginning : refer to situation and purpose

- Middle : detail facts supporting purpose

- Ending : summarise situation and next actions.

EXTERNAL CORRESPONDENCE

LETTERS

BEGINNING

Avoid stilted starts

eg:

- Your correspondence dated ..... is hereby acknowledged

- We are in receipt of your letter dated .....

- We hereby acknowledge

- This letter is written by way of responding to yours dated .....

- We are confirming your letter of

Why not simply say - 'Thank you for your letter dated .....'

SALES MANAGEMENT PARTNERS

1 September 2004

Mr C Dickens
Bleak House
London WC1

Your Reference: CWB/WP123

Dear Mr Dickens

BUSINESS LETTER LAYOUT

Thank you for your fax about the standardised layout of letters. This is to confirm some common mistakes by writers.

The cardinal error is to spell the addressee incorrectly, either in title, company or personal name. This shows a lack of care.

Another problem is the failure to state the writer's purpose early. This frustrates busy readers.

Finally, enclosures are often not numbered. This can lead to confusion when there are a number of enclosures.

The enclosed pocketbook identifies other common problems and solutions.

Yours sincerely

Clive W Bonny
Proprietor

Encl: The Business Writing Pocketbook

cc: Adrian Hunt, Management Pocketbooks

SOUTHVIEW • 8 STONEHILL CLOSE • EAST SHEEN • LONDON SW14 8RP
TELE (0181) 876-1454 • FAX (0181) 878-6970

LETTERS

GIVING BAD NEWS

- Courtesy is crucial - consider their feelings.
- Avoid starting with 'no', judging or blaming.
- When refusing, be clear and say why.
- Help them with alternatives where possible.
- End on a co-operative or sympathetic note.

SALES MANAGEMENT PARTNERS

1 September 2004

Mrs R Jones
East Street
Twickenham
Middlesex

Dear Mrs Jones

<u>**JOB APPLICATION**</u>

Thank you for your letter dated 25 August and your enclosed C.V. Your qualifications are impressive.

We are intending to increase our staff numbers in the future, although not right now.

Regrettably, therefore, we are unable to offer you a position. However, we will keep your details on file for future reference. Thank you for your interest in our company.

Yours sincerely

Clive W Bonny
Proprietor

SOUTHVIEW • 8 STONEHILL CLOSE • EAST SHEEN • LONDON SW14 8RP
TELE (0181) 876-1454 • FAX (0181) 878-6970

EXTERNAL CORRESPONDENCE

LETTERS

COMPLAINTS

- Be **F-I-N-E** when **making** complaints:

  Facts: be specific and factual about who, what, why, when, where

  Implication: describe the effects of the problem

  Needs: say what outcome you want

  End: politely and positively

- When handling complaints show **CUSTOMER** concern

  Concern for clients
  Urgency
  Specific facts
  Timetabled actions
  Options to resolve
  Mailed confirmation
  Empathy for them
  Respect

SALES MANAGEMENT PARTNERS

1 September 2004

For the urgent attention of
Mr Gasket
Service Manager
Crankshaft Garage
Piston Lane
East Sheen, London SW14

Dear Mr Gasket

<u>CAR SERVICE REG NO. ABC 123D .30 AUGUST</u>

I am writing to complain about the condition of my company car following its service. The rear wiper blade was missing.

As I need to reverse into a main road from my driveway, this could result in a major accident.

Can you please fit a new wiper blade when I visit you on Tuesday 6 September? I would expect this free of charge because of the inconvenience. Please phone me on Monday 5 September, 9 - 11am if this is not possible.

Thank you for other work in servicing the car which was of your usual high standard.

Yours sincerely

Mrs V Annoyed
Senior Accountant

SOUTHVIEW • 8 STONEHILL CLOSE • EAST SHEEN • LONDON SW14 8RP
TELE (0181) 876-1454 • FAX (0181) 878-6970

EXTERNAL CORRESPONDENCE

LETTERS

INFLUENCING TO WIN A SALES APPOINTMENT

The strategy is to get **A I D A** to **C I Am** in **Need**

Attention	- focus on you the reader	**C**ircumstances
Interest	- identifying with the readers	**I**ssues
Desire	- stimulating readers' wants	**Am**ount to
Action	- by whom and by when	**Need**

SALES MANAGEMENT PARTNERS

1 September 2004

Mrs S Brown
NewPro Limited
The Innovation Centre
Bracknell
Berkshire

Dear Mrs Brown

COMPANY EXPANSION WITH NEW PRODUCTS

Your press release in The Times last week caught my eye. You announced that your new products will catapult you into market leadership within 2 years.

I believe that you can achieve this earlier than forecast, and I would like to meet you to show how this may be accomplished.

Other companies like your own have found my information has helped them achieve their strategic goals and increase market share. Bill Smith of AB & Co suggested I contacted you directly. I am not sure at this stage how helpful I can be to you and a brief meeting would establish this quickly.

Can we meet on Thursday 8 September, 8.30 a.m. at your office? Alternatively, should this be inconvenient, I could rearrange a more suitable time through your personal assistant.

I will call you on Monday to discuss further.

Yours sincerely

Clive W Bonny
Proprietor

SOUTHVIEW • 8 STONEHILL CLOSE • EAST SHEEN • LONDON SW14 8RP
TELE (0181) 876-1454 • FAX (0181) 878-6970

LETTERS TO CUSTOMERS

EXERCISE

Check your policy and procedures:

- How quickly should I reply? Is this achieved? When I cannot answer queries quickly am I sending interim acknowledgements?

- How tidy and up to date are my customer correspondence files?

- How do I check the impression my letter makes?

- Who handles correspondence in my absence?

EXTERNAL CORRESPONDENCE

PROPOSALS

DRAFTING

- Submit a **DRAFT** first to check what your reader wants.
- Test the draft with your 'inside' supporter.
- If competing with others, submit your draft **LAST** - then ask how it compares with others.
- Submit it **IN PERSON** to verify acceptability.
- Give **COST OPTIONS**, breaking costs down into smaller terms,
    eg: cost per day **NOT** per year
       cost per item **NOT** per shipment.

COVERING LETTERS

- Personalise for each recipient
- Thank them for any help given
- Put a deadline on any quotation
- Confirm next action (**NOT** 'we await your reply')

EXTERNAL CORRESPONDENCE

PROPOSALS
STRUCTURE

1. Covering Letter, outlining benefits.
2. Management Summary, key points proposed.
3. Client Aims and Objectives, company-wide and departmental.
4. Current Methods and Costs, identifying their concerns.
5. Requirements: New conditions, Needs and Priorities.
6. Proposed Improvements and implications.
7. Implementation Plan, with simple steps: how, who, when, where.
8. Supplier's Unique Benefits, as wanted by the client.
9. Cost-benefits and return on Investment, counterbalancing costs.
10. Appendices, detailing supporting information.

EXTERNAL CORRESPONDENCE

PROPOSALS

FORMAT

SAY 'YOU'

USE HEADINGS

CREATE WHITE SPACE

SHORTEN PARAGRAPHS

DOUBLE SPACE LINES

INSERT GRAPHICS

PUT CAPTIONS ON GRAPHICS

EMPHASISE WITH UNDERLINING, *ITALICS*, **BOLDFACE**

MAKE YOUR WEB SITE WORK

- Make it interactive and easy to navigate
- Integrate messages with appealing visuals
- Encourage reader response
- Monitor effectiveness
- Show case studies of your offer (visit www.consult-smp.com for examples)
- Use colours to create emotive effects:
  - red or yellow to excite
  - blue or green to calm

EXTERNAL CORRESPONDENCE

MAKE YOUR WEB SITE WORK
PUBLISH CASE STUDIES OF SUCCESS

A good case study describes:

- How you helped improve a situation
- Why change was required
- Who was involved
- How quickly improvements occurred
- What specific benefits arose
- Why you were chosen to help

PERSONALISING

PERSONALISING

ADDRESS THE READER

There is one word which arouses more attention than any other: **OUR NAME**.

The next most interesting words are closely associated:

YOU - YOUR - YOURS. So...

- Write from the reader's viewpoint.

- Address their needs and wants.

- Say 'What's in it for them?'.

- Use language which fits what the readers **ASK**

Attitude -	their values and expectations
Status -	their position and responsibility
Knowledge -	their ability to understand you

PERSONALISING

LANGUAGE

Our language has grown over the years.

Here are some LANGUAGE STATISTICS:

Shakespeare used 17,677 different words in his complete works.

The first English Dictionary in 1755 defined 43,000 words.

There are now nearly half a million words in the Oxford English Dictionary. English is used by 360 million people as a first language and by over a billion people as a second language.

American Paul Dickson found 2,231 words and phrases to express one word 'intoxication',

eg: plastered, overloaded, blotto, cockeyed, embalmed.

Words can have many meanings. As language expands so do the chances of misunderstanding!

Over five million people in Britain have sub-standard writing.

PERSONALISING

PRECISION

Exercise

Write down your understanding   1) Soon
of these words in NUMERICAL   2) High
terms: 3) Fast
                                4) Long

Now ask your customers or colleagues to do the same and compare results.

- Is 'soon' minutes, hours, days?
- Is 'high' inches, feet, miles?
- Is 'fast' time or speed?
- Is 'long' time or distance?

When you say 'as soon as possible' to someone, check you both know what it really means!

PERSONALISING

STYLE

BE F A B

- Convert **F**eatures into **A**dvantages and **B**enefits for the reader

- Convert I and We into You

- Convert Nouns into Verbs

and keep it short and simple **K I S S**

Exercise: Be **F A B & K I S S** this example:

Our proficient IT specialists in DTP could facilitate the production of data transference onto hard copy to generate improvements in mailshots.

Please refer to the next page to improve the style.

PERSONALISING

STYLE

● Improve the previous page by explaining jargon

from
'Our proficient IT specialists in DTP':

to
'our experts in Desk Top Publishing'

● Shorten long words

from
'facilitate the production of data transference onto hard copy'

to
'help in writing'

'to generate improvements in mailshots'

'write better letters'

Example improved:

'you will write better letters with the help of our experts in Desk Top Publishing'.

54

PERSONALISING

TONE

Remember your **A B C**

Actively Be Courteous

Exercise: Improve the following examples:

1) To A. Hunt

   We are running a training workshop in customer-orientated written communication skills for all new employees. Register below for inclusion herewith.

2) Dear Sir/Madam

   Our company trading terms now stipulate a 5% deposit must be transmitted for all orders to be expedited in a maximum seven days.

PERSONALISING

TONE

TIPS

Talk about you (ie: the reader).

Check their names in advance if possible.

Use the **Active** not **Passive** tense

eg:

from Passive	**to Active**
the goods were ordered by the customer	the customer ordered the goods
'notice is hereby given'	'we are advising'

What is your version of the two examples, using **FAB, KISS AND ABC**?

Please refer to the next page to check your tone.

PERSONALISING

TONE
EXAMPLES IMPROVED

1) Adrian,
   You are warmly invited to improve your skills in writing to your customers.
   Please sign your name below. We look forward to seeing you.
2) Dear Mrs Jones,
   Your 5% deposit will ensure that, complying with our new terms, you will
   receive your orders within a week.

Don't write with not too many negatives - it's confusing!

SOUND POSITIVE : WRITE SAYING Y E S
from	to
● 'We cannot supply before May 13 ...'	● 'You can secure our services after May 12 ..'
● 'a not inopportune moment'	● 'a convenient time'
● 'you have not yet responded'	● 'please reply'
● 'you failed to enclose'	● 'please send'
● 'if'	● 'when'
● 'but	● 'and'
● 'could'	● 'can'

Whenever possible
start and end with a
THANK YOU.

57

PERSONALISING

SEXISM

It is difficult to recognise sexual bias in our own writing, even when it is obvious to others.

Using 'he' when the gender is unknown can cause offence.

Improve from

to

'*Policemen* will be available'

'Police *officers* will be available'

or just '*Police* will be available'

'We must elect a *Chairman*'

'We must elect *someone to chair* .....'

or 'We must elect a *chairperson* .....'

'A doctor likes time with *his* patients'

'A doctor likes time with *the* patient'

or 'Doctors like time with *their* patients'

PERSONALISING

OFFICIALESE

Avoid officialese

Instead of:
The duly accepted forms should be submitted to the undersigned upon completion.

Try:
Please return the signed forms when you have completed them.

N.B.   The passive verb '**be submitted**' is also now an active verb in '**return**'.

Active verbs give **LIFE** to dull text.

LANGUAGE TYPES

Research shows that certain personality types prefer certain words.

Dominant people prefer words answering **'WHAT?'** with decisive outcomes, eg: results, goals, accomplishments.
This type likes words which are businesslike, functional and to the point.

Expressive people prefer words answering **'WHO?'** with emotional spontaneity, eg: great, new, vision, status.
This type likes words which are creative, informal and fast-paced.

Supportive people prefer words answering **'HOW?'** with friendly empathy, eg: service, standards, understanding, involvement.
This type likes words which are easy to use, slower paced, and chosen with feeling.

Cautious people prefer words answering **'WHY?'** with detailed accuracy, eg: facts and figures, analysis, logic.
This type likes words which are precise, formal and well planned.

MATCH LANGUAGE TO TYPE

Example statements to match their 'types':

DOMINANT
'This is an opportunity for you to decide for yourself in only a few minutes. You will see and get credit for the fast financial returns.'

EXPRESSIVE
'Your vision to build on your team's great success and expand into new areas will be applauded by everyone'.

SUPPORTIVE
'I will show you how others have found this process to be a reliable and secure way of involving their colleagues.'

CAUTIOUS
'This process has been thoroughly researched. All supporting data is attached, proving that quality standards can be maintained.'

PERSONALISING

EXERCISE

How to check your personal styles:

Choose 1 word in each horizontal row which describes you best.

1	**2**	**3**	**4**
driving	talkative	patient	conventional
ambitious	magnetic	reliable	neat
pioneering	enthusiastic	deliberate	conservative
forceful	persuasive	loyal	perfectionist
determined	trusting	dependable	careful
goal-oriented	friendly	consistent	cautious
competitive	demonstrative	steady	exacting
decisive	optimistic	stable	systematic
strongwilled	polished	relaxed	precise
independent	sociable	modest	compliant

TOTAL The words in each vertical column

Your preferences are as follows:

Column 1   is for Dominant people   3   is for Supportive people

        2   is for Expressive people   4   is for Cautious people

VHF WORDS

Many of us also have preferences for words with a bias for either:
Visualising   Hearing   or Feeling

Visualising:
I *see* what you mean   we *pictured* the scene   they *eyed* me up

Hearing:
I *listened* intently   we *sounded* them out   they *voiced* their opinions

Feeling:
I *grasped* the point   we *picked* up the meaning   they *touched* a nerve

You can identify someone's preference in **VHF** language by listening to their speech and by examining their writing. Tune into the wavelengths of your customers, your boss and your colleagues by selecting **their** VHF channel.

They will pick up your signals more clearly!

PERSONALISING

VHF EXERCISE

Do you have preferences? For each word in the General Meaning column, mark the V, H or F equivalent which you are most likely to use. Count the number of marks per column. You may see a clear preference for one channel or a more even distribution.

GENERAL MEANING	V	H	F
attitude	viewpoint	comment	stance
consider	look over	sound out	put feelers out
persevere with	see through	hear out	stick with
demonstrate	show	explain	sort out
plain	lack-lustre	muted	dull
be attentive	keep an eye on	listen to	care for
ignore	overlook	tune out	pass over
go over	look over	talk over	run through
identify	point out	call attention	to put a finger on
remind one of	look familiar	ring a bell	strike
repeat	review	rehearse	rerun
refer to	point to	allude to	touch upon
insensitive	blind	deaf	unfeeling
reflect	mirror	echo	bounce
balance	symmetry	harmony	tranquillity
learned	pictured	clicked with	got a grip of

PRESENTING

PRESENTING

DISPLAY OPTIONS

Visual displays give your writing impact.
Most of us remember pictures more easily than words or numbers.
It is also easier to interpret figures shown pictorially.

- **Bar Charts** help to compare changes in relative quantity.

- **Line graphs** help to show trends and moving averages over time
  to plan and forecast.

- **Pie Charts** help you see proportions of a whole.

- **Pictograms** show pictorial symbols of statistics.

- **Organograms** show reporting relationships between people in organisations.

DISPLAY OPTIONS
TIPS FOR CHARTS AND GRAPHS

- Keep them simple and use the full axis space.

- Use colour or 3 D.

- Label them and cross reference with the text.

  Bar charts should have no more than twelve bars.

  Pie charts should have no more than eight sections.

  Line graphs should have no more than four line types.

  Label axes clearly, placing **TIME** horizontally.

BAR CHARTS

Use: Compares quantities in columns using vertical bars.

Tips: Separate columns; keep one scale.

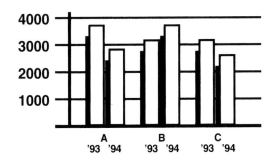

PIE CHARTS

Use: Shows proportions of a whole, usually in percentages.
             Effective for up to eight component parts.

Tips: Use colour coding and consistent typefaces.

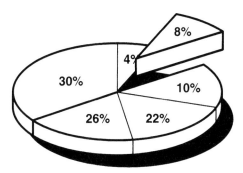

LINE GRAPHS

Use: Shows flow of quantities rising and falling over time.

Tips: Put quantities on vertical (y) axis.
                 Put time on horizontal (x) axis.
                 Use up to three graph lines with different colours.

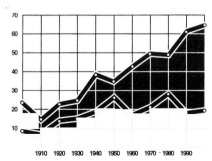

PRESENTING

TABLES

Use: Compares exact numbers or words in columns.

Tips: Put illustrations to describe subjects.
Make sure all figures/words are legible.

	Price	Number	Percent
Place 1	£500	150	10.5%
Place 2	£650	120	8.0%
Place 3	£550	165	5.5%
Place 4	£450	100	8.5%
Place 5	£750	125	7.0%
Place 6	£600	130	12.0%

PRESENTING

GANTT CHARTS

These are horizontal bar charts that use straight lines to show the timing of steps in a project, and the sequence of activities underway one at a time.

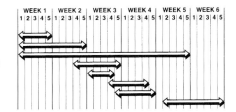

TASK DESCRIPTION

1. DECIDE WHO SHOULD ATTEND
2. INVESTIGATE POSSIBLE VENUES
3. DESIGN COURSE
4. DETERMINE ATTENDEES' AVAILABILITY
5. AGREE SUITABLE DATE
6. BOOK VENUE
7. INVITE PARTICIPANTS
8. TEST COURSE

GANTT CHARTS
IMPLEMENTATION

Here is an example flow chart of how to **implement** the GANTT chart.

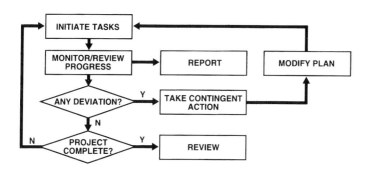

PRESENTING

PERT DIAGRAMS

PERT stands for   **P**rogramme
Evaluation &
Review
Technique

Appropriate for projects with many interactive steps.

There are usually 5 components:

EVENTS	— shown by circles
ACTIVITIES	— lines or arrows connecting circles
NON-ACTIVITIES	— dotted lines or arrows showing event dependencies, where no work is needed
TIMEFRAMES	— estimated and actual time of tasks
CRITICAL PATH	— showing essential steps for completion.

PERT DIAGRAMS
ILLUSTRATION

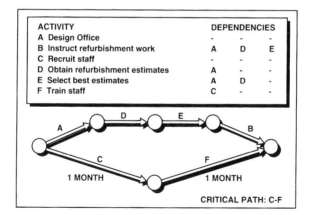

ACTIVITY	DEPENDENCIES		
A Design Office	-	-	-
B Instruct refurbishment work	A	D	E
C Recruit staff	-	-	-
D Obtain refurbishment estimates	A	-	-
E Select best estimates	A	D	-
F Train staff	C	-	-

CRITICAL PATH: C-F

ORGANOGRAM

Use: Illustrates relationships and presents information in an organised, inter-connected form.

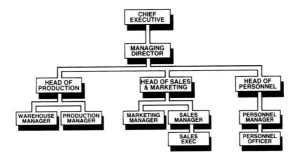

PRESENTING

TRICKERY

Statistics can deceive what the eyes perceive. Watch out for pictorial dishonesty.
Common tricks include:
- using different bar chart widths
- inverting axis points, eg: Jan - Dec - Nov
- changing the numbers on axis points: 0 10 50 100
- rounding upwards
- smoothing out moving averages
- quoting averages as:

MEAN — adding the numbers then dividing by the number of numbers.
MEDIAN — the mid-point.   **MODE** — the most common number

eg: Sales Turnover by Salesperson:

Andy.......... 65	Belinda ..... 71 (mode)
Charles...... 71	Daisy.......... 91
Eric............ 93 (median)	Fiona........ 109
George......138	Harry........ 300 (mean)
Jane.......... 600	

Belinda and Eric claimed to have average figures.

PUTTING IDEAS ON PAPER
BRAINSTORMING

We respond more readily to the word when **written** than when spoken.

VISUAL stimulus allows the brain to focus on and enlarge a key point in the **mind's eye.**

Process

1) Write the issue clearly and concisely on a blank sheet of flipchart paper.

2) Invite a group of people to say anything that comes to mind and record the words on the flipchart, keeping all words visible to the group.

3) Encourage them all to contribute any ideas without judging, criticising or stopping the flow for 5 - 15 minutes.

4) Stop and sift words into groups linking associated words on single sheet diagrams.

5) Hang out 'to dry' in view of contributors for a few days.

6) Repeat the brainstorm to add new ideas.

7) Prioritise and agree best options.

PUTTING IDEAS ON PAPER
AIDS TO DECISION-MAKING

Different ways of presenting information on paper can be of great assistance in making judgments and reaching decisions. Combinations of words trigger new associations; different groupings highlight hidden connections.

- **FORCE FIELD ANALYSIS**

  Make 2 vertical lists: Forces 'For' versus Forces 'Against'

  This links relative strengths and weaknesses

- **FISHBONE diagrams** link cause and effect

  Write the cause of the problem as the backbone

```
                    effects on          People              Process
CENTRAL ——————— CAUSE ——————— OF ——————— PROBLEM
                    effects on          equipment           materials
```

PRESENTING

PUTTING IDEAS ON PAPER
AIDS TO DECISION-MAKING (Cont'd)

● REVERSAL STATEMENT

This reverses the issue statement to create a new perspective, eg: from 'How can I visit new business prospects?' to 'How can new business prospects visit me?'

● BUG LIST

This develops two lists: LIKES AND DISLIKES, to help decide actions.

● SPIDERGRAM

This helps to develop lines of thought.

EXAMPLE OF A SPIDERGRAM

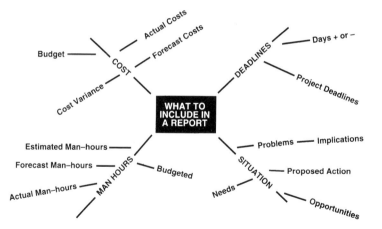

MIND MAPS FOR PERSONAL NOTE-TAKING

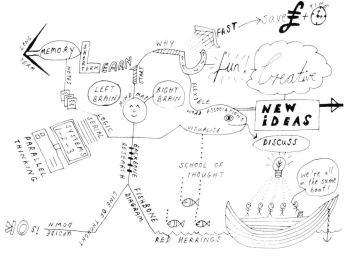

MIND MAPS FOR PERSONAL NOTE-TAKING

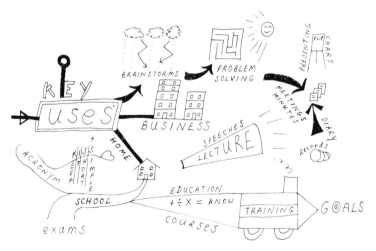

MIND MAPPING
RULES OF THUMB

- Start in the centre of a blank page

- PRINT words, one per line
  Highlight and link with lines, circles and squares

- Colour code and draw pictures and symbols

- Abbreviate

MIND MAPPING

EXERCISE

Now practise by drawing a mind map about yourself.

Alternatively, download free of charge mind map software from www.mindjet.de

PERSONAL HANDWRITING

The scientific study of handwriting is called GRAPHOLOGY and is used by many businesses to help determine the personality traits of potential employees.

Its basis is that once we learn how to write, we develop our own unique style which spontaneously reflects our subconscious mind.

Its most popular business use is in recruitment, where recruiters will ask for applicants to send in handwritten details of themselves.

The main areas examined by graphologists are the four S's:

S tyle (general)
S hape of letter
S pacing
S ignature.

HANDWRITING

ACCEPTABLE

Characteristics favoured by graphologists for general commercial duties are:

Style:
- regular in size, with clear vertical strokes
- whole lines written horizontally or sloping slightly upwards
- numbers especially legible.

Shape of Letter:
- rounded for people-oriented jobs
- angular for task-oriented jobs
- **i dotted and t crossed** towards the right
- **small d** sloping slightly right.

i

t

d

Spacing:
- equally well-spaced between words and lines
- moderate left side margin.

Signature:
- clear and firmly written
- little flourish except for a single underline
- slightly larger than ordinary writing.

HANDWRITING
LESS ACCEPTABLE

Graphological signs considered UNFAVOURABLE for general commercial duties are the opposite of those previously mentioned, particularly:

Style:
- irregular or backward sloping words
- whole lines written in downward slope
- elaborate flourishes, or more than 2 strokes on figures.

Shape of Letter
- a and o open at the bottom
- t bars omitted or sloping down
- i dots omitted or placed left of centre
- d looped over other letters at the top

a o t i
chaotic!

Spacing:
- excessive, irregular or insufficient.

Signature:
- corkscrew finish underneath
- reversing wavy line underneath
- loop surrounding name.

MARKETING COMMUNICATIONS

MARKETING COMMUNICATIONS

FIRST IMPRESSIONS

Packaging is important.
Create positive first impressions with the right:

- **colour** of envelope - white not brown

- **address** - neatly handwritten not labelled

- **feel** - heavier quality paper (100 gm)

- **fold** - twice horizontally. 1/3 and 2/3 down on an A4 page.

MARKETING COMMUNICATIONS

STATIONERY

BUSINESS STATIONERY can promote our services with the help of:

- a **LOGO** - people remember pictures (frank your envelopes with a logo)
- a **MOTTO** - people remember rhymes
- a **SLOGAN** - people remember catchphrases
- a **BUSINESS NAME** describing your offer

Use quality paper with fold markers.

Have business cards which 'stand out'.

MARKETING COMMUNICATIONS

GENERAL STRATEGY

ATTENTION	:	put a benefit in the headline
INTEREST	:	make it personal and topical
DESIRE	:	expand benefits with 'word-pictures'
CONVICTION	:	prove benefits with testimonials and referrals
ACTION	:	ask for action and justify **fast** action.

DIRECT MAIL

Use POSITIVE **WORD-POWER**

Some words catch our attention quickly

eg:

YOU	UNIQUE
SAVE	EXCLUSIVE
NEW	SECRET
PROVEN	SAFETY
OFFER	DISCOVER
YES	NOW
SALE	HEALTHY

MARKETING COMMUNICATIONS

DIRECT MAILSHOT

OBJECTIVE: to generate enquiries

The letter:

- Address to a named person, not Sir/Madam
- State main benefit to them
- Quote testimonial/proof statement
- Prompt action now in a PS
- Sign it
- Use bold caps to highlight key words
- Enclose a reply card or a pre-addressed window envelope

MARKETING COMMUNICATIONS

DIRECT RESPONSE ADVERTISING

Positioning is all important on the page:

EXAMPLE showing the sequence of where readers' eyes travel

1. PICTURE

2. HEADLINE / BENEFIT

3. CAPTION / PROOF STATEMENT

6. DETAILS / FEATURES

4. RESPONSE COUPON / INCENTIVE

5. OFFER

MARKETING COMMUNICATIONS

DIRECT RESPONSE OFFERS

FOR THE BEST
MARKETING
TALK TO US!

Here are twelve proven ways of winning direct responses.

Include a :

- gift offer
- free trial
- free survey
- free sample
- trade-in offer
- refund Certificate

- moneyback guarantee
- bill later
- cash discount
- limited time offer
- price increase notice
- sweepstake

MARKETING COMMUNICATIONS

ADVERTISING COPY

Positioning is Paramount in the press.

More responses come from these media positions:

>   FRONT PAGE
>   BACK PAGE
>   INSIDE FRONT
>   INSIDE BACK
>   (and near leisure pages in local press)

but they are usually more expensive!

MARKETING COMMUNICATIONS

ADVERTORIAL

Businesses can write their own advertising copy in **EDITORIAL** style to give an air of objectivity and to supply more information.

This 'Advertorial' style should be similar to Press Release copy (see page 99).

It must be clearly marked **'ADVERTISEMENT'**.

This is especially effective when printed alongside a normal advertisement to increase reader response.

MARKETING COMMUNICATIONS

PRESS RELEASES

These can create readership awareness at much lower cost than advertising.
They are also more credible than direct sales offers - because they are perceived
by readers as objective and accurate descriptions.

- Select a theme which is topical and newsworthy

- Summarise your story in the first paragraph

- Ensure text answers all questions
  (Who? What? When? Where? Why?)

- Use quotations but avoid exaggeration

- Write it in the third person (not 'we have' but 'the firm has')

- Use a subject heading which attracts readers

- Keep the length to a single page

MARKETING COMMUNICATIONS

PRESS RELEASES

- Address it to the journalist by name

- Add your name and contact details

- Date it

- Use double space lines and wide margins

- Enclose a photograph with a brief caption attached

MARKETING COMMUNICATIONS

PRESS RELEASES

DON'T:

- Start sentences with numbers
- Use italics, upper case, very large or small type faces
- Underline or abbreviate
- Be humorous!

Example: How NOT to start:

'I would like to invite you to immerse yourself in the world of the herpes simplex virus'.

(from Private Eye)

PRESS RELEASE

Release Date   12 November 2004

COMPUTER SOLUTIONS COMPANY WINS NATIONAL TRAINING AWARD

An Oxfordshire based business has been granted the prestigious national training accolade of becoming an 'Investor In People' AB & Co of Chinnor have been recognised by the Training and Enterprise Council for their Quality systems and practices to develop their employees.

They join only a handful of other computer service companies in achieving this James Jones, Managing Director, says '**This helps us give a first class service to our customers. Staff who feel cared for will show care for our customers**'.

The company also qualified for funded consultancy support from Sales Management Partners whose Proprietor, Clive Bonny, said '**Many businesses like AB & Co can improve their effectiveness through Investors In People. My role is to help show them how**'.

For further information contact Clive Bonny, Sales Management Partners, 8 Stonehill Close, East Sheen, London, SW14 8RP
Telephone 0181-876-1454 Fax: 0181-878-6970.

ENDS

ENCLOSED: One black and white photo with caption reading 'James Jones receives the award from Mr Smith, Chairman of the Training and Enterprise Council'.

MARKETING COMMUNICATIONS

CHECKLIST
FOR ADVERTISING, BROCHURES AND DIRECT MAIL

HAVE YOU:

- Appealed to what interests the reader most?

- Clearly stated what you offer and what it will do for the reader?

- Used short words, short sentences and short paragraphs?

- Made it visually attractive?

- Motivated readers to respond quickly and easily?

MARKETING COMMUNICATIONS

USING THE INTERNET

DO:

- Be courteous - 'netiquette'
- Respect intellectual property
- Consider cultural differences

DON'T:

- Share your password
- Copy everyone
- Violate libel law

CHECKING

CHECKING

SPEED READING

A reading speed of 200-300 words per minute is considered average. Many of us can DOUBLE this speed without losing the meaning of the text.

This means HALVING the time spent on reading. If we read for only 50 minutes a day, then saving 25 minutes a day adds up to over 8 hours every month.

Speed reading is **not** scanning. Scanning results in missing mistakes; proper speed reading picks them up. **Plus**, laying out your written material in a format which enables speed readers to absorb it quickly will help convey your message.

SPEED-READING TIPS

First, calculate how many words you normally read in a minute.

Put the page on a flat surface within easy reach. Keep your elbows tucked in and your head still. Use a 'pointer' with a finger or a pen.

Using your 'pointer' develop a steady rhythm of moving it across the page. Don't stop, retrace the same words or say them out loud.

Apply different 'conductor' styles for different styles of text, letting your eye follow the tip of the 'pointer' picking up key words (eg: nouns and verbs).

SPEED READING

For Newspapers:
Start left to right to the end of the line then skip a line down and move the pointer right to left

→ →
← ←

For business articles:
move the pointer only in the middle section of the text

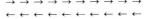

For technical writing:
move the pointer left to right across the full line, and concentrate on the first and last sentences in each paragraph.

Keep practising by setting improvement goals in your speed and comprehension.

Eventually you will be able to read entire blocks of words diagonally downwards and upwards.

CHECKING

PLAIN ENGLISH

Why do we write gobbledegook?
We are often taught it at school!

EXAMPLE:

PGCE English Major Assignment

a) in 1,000 words construct a justified model of English in the secondary school;
    you should refer to the National Curriculum and its provenance, and whatever
    writers you judge as relevant; eg: Leavis, Holbrook, Eagleton, Britton, et al.

b) in 500 words give a trenchant account of observed reality in the teaching of
    English in your Autumn term school.

The marking criteria are not mechanical but discourse related; each section of this
assignment should be distinctive in terms of the rubric above.

Written by a College of Education

AVOID BUSINESS JARGON

from	to
down-sizing	reducing
de-manning	losing jobs
hands-on	practical
state of the art	new
interface with	discuss
input	entry
normalise	return to normal
scenario	plan
put on the back burner	put off
user-friendly	easy to use
IT	information technology

down-sizing

CHECKING

AVOID 'DOUBLE ENTRY'

from	to
viable alternative	alternative
revert back	revert
past history	past
forward planning	planning
end result	result
added bonus	bonus
particularly distinct	distinct
free gift	gift
of limited availability	limited
crisis situation	crisis
previous experience	experience
9 a.m. in the morning	9 a.m.
empty vacancy	vacancy
seldom ever	seldom
actual fact	fact
unexpected surprise	surprise

CHECKING

CLARITY
THE FOG FACTOR

Take a typical sample of about 200 words of your writing.
Count the number of sentences. Count all words with 3 or more syllables
(eg: cla-ri-ty has 3) excluding personal pronouns (names).

Then apply the FOG FACTOR:

Divide the number of long words by the number of sentences.
Clear writing has a fog factor of between 2 & 3.

Below 2 may be childishly simple.

Above 3 may be DISTINCTLY FOGGY!

CLARITY
THE CLOZE TEST

If you must include long words in your writing apply the Cloze Test for clarity.

Take a sample about 250 words long.

Delete the 36th word, and then every 10th word.

Then read it to a colleague. If they cannot give you a suitable replacement word for at least 3 in every 4 deletions then your writing is unclear.

CLARITY

Use K I S S (Keep It Short and Simple)

by turning nouns to verbs.

From:

utilisation of the computer in payroll preparation
will bring about a reduction in clerical costs.

To:

using the computer to prepare payrolls will reduce clerical costs.

CLARITY

Can you simplify this example?

Extract from a British telephone directory:

> 'A spot check of randomly selected directories indicated that
> a number of the directories contained several blank pages.
>
> In view of the foregoing it is suggested that each user review the issue
> directory and ascertain whether or not the directory is complete.
>
> In the event that the directory is incomplete, the user should return the
> directory to the issue source for disposal.'

Try this:

'If you have blank pages in your directory please return it'.

CHECKING

FOR SHORT SENTENCES
CREATE ONE IDEA PER SENTENCE

EXAMPLE: FROM TWO IDEAS

The Administration Manager has requested the installation of an additional unit at your address for the purpose of providing extra facilities for the staff in that area.

Into two SEPARATE SENTENCES

The Administration Manager has requested the installation of an additional unit at your address. Its purpose will be to provide extra facilities for the staff in that area.

KEEP IT SIMPLE

Use short words to avoid 'extended endings'

eg: ..... ise

from	to
visualise	see
utilise	use
marginalise	set aside

..... ate

compensate	pay
terminate	end
facilitate	help

..... able

applicable	apply
attributable	due
considerable	much

CHECKING

'REDUNDANT' PHRASES

Many of these phrases are used automatically. A single word is often more powerful.

Eg:

at a later date	later
in the event that	if
due to the fact that	because
take into consideration	consider
for the purpose of	for
with reference to	about
come to a conclusion	conclude
make a decision	decide
submit a proposal	propose

CHECKING

'REDUNDANT' WORDS

Cut out words like:

- on the grounds that
- in view of
- for the reason that
- inasmuch as
- in consequence of
- owing to the fact that
- apart from the fact that
- on account of
- consequently due to
- in the light of

Take the short cut, simply say

'BECAUSE'

GRAMMAR

The English language without grammar would be like a jigsaw puzzle without a picture guide. Put another way, what confusing for readers are is not having no chance words understanding.

Here are examples of other mistakes:

● Two or more ideas in a single sentence

eg: 'We will grow market share with an increase in sales agents and the business plan must be shared with all senior managers'.

Split this into two sentences by stopping at 'agents': 'and' then becomes 'Also' or 'Additionally'.

● Phrases which dangle at the wrong end of a sentence

eg: 'After travelling all day, Aberdeen came into sight'.
This should read: 'After travelling all day, we saw Aberdeen'.

CHECKING

LANGUAGE

Watch out for:

- **'mixed metaphors'**: here are some 'real life' dummies!
  Eg: 'Our business has been teetering on the edge for some time, and now is the time to move forward'.

    OR

'You can't beat the tidal wave when the avalanche comes down the mountain'.

- **oxymorons:**   Word combinations which contradict themselves:
  eg: pretty ugly   perfectly terrible
  deafening silence   distinctly foggy.

- **puns:**   Words which amuse with their play on meaning:
  eg: we saw that axing this idea was the only way to hammer the competitors.

- **spoonerisms:**   Words which are mixed up, eg: from 'managing dual agents' to 'damaging mule agents'.

LANGUAGE

- **homonyms**
  Words with the same sound and spelling but different meaning:

  eg: 'Terms to Watch' (we really mean 'English expressions to avoid')

- **logograms**
  Signs that substitute words, and can be mis-read:

  eg: &   *for* and
       //   *for* number
       +   *for* in addition
       —   *for* less

- **malapropisms**
  Words which incorrectly resemble the right words:
  eg: 'The tasty meal went down in the anals of gastronomy'.

CLICHÉS

Clichés are over-used expressions.

Eg: water under the bridge   to all intents and purposes
        stick to our guns   moving the goalposts
        painstaking investigation   package of measures
        leaving no stone unturned   keeping our heads above water
        fingers in every pie   at this point in time

Don't be lazy - find alternatives. Avoid tired phrases like the following:

from	to
herewith please find enclosed	I enclose .....
we hereby acknowledge	Thank you
It is our own opinion	I believe
if you have any queries, please do not hesitate to contact this office	Should you have any questions please contact me

SPELLING

Spelling mistakes make sloppy impressions.

EXERCISE: CORRECT ANY MIS-SPELLINGS

1	accessible	18	fulfill	35	questionaire
2	accomodation	19	feasability	36	proceedure
3	acknowledge	20	grievence	37	reccomend
4	assesment	21	guarantee	38	remittence
5	benefitted	22	imminent	39	reference
6	calandor	23	incomparible	40	relevence
7	changable	24	independant	41	separate
8	conveniance	25	liason	42	serviceable
9	commitee	26	maintainance	43	successfull
10	correspondance	27	neccessary	44	supercede
11	definately	28	occassionally	45	tarriff
12	delapidated	29	omitted	46	tendancy
13	developement	30	parallel	47	temporary
14	dissatisfied	31	permanent	48	transferable
15	elligible	32	permissable	49	truely
16	efficiency	33	persue	50	withold
17	emergancy	34	preparation		

(see page 126)

CHECKING

SIGN MISTAKES

AMEND

Notice in health food shop window:

CLOSED DUE TO ILLNESS

In a department store:

BARGAIN BASEMENT UPSTAIRS

In a laundromat:

AUTOMATIC WASHING MACHINES PLEASE REMOVE ALL YOUR CLOTHES WHEN THE LIGHT GOES OUT

Spotted in a safari park:

ELEPHANTS PLEASE STAY IN YOUR CAR

In an office:

WOULD THE PERSON WHO TOOK THE STEP LADDER YESTERDAY PLEASE BRING IT BACK OR FURTHER STEPS WILL BE TAKEN

In an office WC:

TOILET OUT OF ORDER - PLEASE USE FLOOR BELOW

CHECKING

SPELLING CORRECTIONS

2	accommodation	17	emergency
4	assessment	18	fulfil
5	benefited	19	feasibility
6	calendar	20	grievance
7	changeable	23	incomparable
8	convenience	24	independent
9	committee	25	liaison
10	correspondence	26	maintenance
11	definitely	27	necessary
12	dilapidated	28	occasionally
13	development	32	permissible
15	eligible	33	pursue

35	questionnaire
36	procedure
37	recommend
38	remittance
40	relevance
43	successful
45	tariff
46	tendency
49	truly
50	withhold

About the Author

Clive W. Bonny

Clive's early career began in financial services management. It progressed through accounting and marketing into direct sales with British, German and American employers. His sales career developed into major accounts and sales management within commercial, central government and local government sectors, consistently breaking company sales records for new business. He was appointed General Manager in a publicly quoted American multi-national company with profit and loss responsibility and within a two year period he improved divisional net profits from 6.8% to 18.2% of total revenues whilst increasing the customer base tenfold.

Clive is owner-manager of Strategic Management Partners, advising organisations on Business Excellence and coaching individuals to improve results. Besides success in operational and board level positions, he is a Certified Management Consultant, a Fellow of the RSA, and author of several publications on corporate communications, career management and business ethics.

Contact

Clive can be contacted at: Strategic Management Partners, Magnolia House, 33 Berwyn Road, Richmond, Surrey TW10 5BP. Tel: 0208 876 4211 Fax: 0208 274 0148 Mobile: 07973-799153 www.consult-smp.com

Success Breeds Success when Values Sustain Value

© Clive W. Bonny 1994
This edition published in 1994 by Management Pocketbooks Ltd.
Laurel House, Station Approach, Alresford, Hants SO24 9JH, U.K.

Reprinted 1996, 1998, 2000, 2002, 2004, 2005, 2007. Printed in UK.   ISBN 978 1 870471 22 0

ORDER FORM

Your details

Name _____

Position _____

Company _____

Address _____

_____

_____

Telephone _____

Fax _____

E-mail _____

VAT No. (EC companies) _____

Your Order Ref _____

Please send me:

		No. copies
The Business Writing	Pocketbook	
The _____	Pocketbook	
The _____	Pocketbook	
The _____	Pocketbook	
The _____	Pocketbook	

Order by Post

MANAGEMENT POCKETBOOKS LTD

LAUREL HOUSE, STATION APPROACH,
ALRESFORD, HAMPSHIRE SO24 9JH UK

Order by Phone, Fax or Internet

Telephone: +44 (0)1962 735573
Facsimile: +44 (0)1962 733637
E-mail: sales@pocketbook.co.uk
Web: www.pocketbook.co.uk

MANAGEMENT POCKETBOOKS